EMP

16 SIMPLE HABITS TO PROTECT YOURSELF, FEEL BETTER & ENJOY LIFE EVEN IF YOU ARE HIGHLY SENSITIVE

VIK CARTER

Disclaimer

The information herein is offered for informational purposes solely, and is universal as so. The presentation of the information is without contract or any type of guarantee assurance.

This document is geared towards providing exact and reliable information in regards to the topic and issue covered. The publication is sold with the idea that the publisher is not required to render accounting, officially permitted, or otherwise, qualified services. If advice is necessary, legal or professional, a practiced individual in the profession should be ordered.

From a Declaration of Principles which was accepted and approved equally by a Committee of the American Bar Association and a Committee of Publishers and Associations. In no way is it legal to reproduce, duplicate, or transmit any part of this document in either electronic means or in printed format. Recording of this publication is strictly prohibited and any storage of this document is not allowed unless with written permission from the publisher. All rights reserved.

The information provided herein is stated to be truthful and consistent, in that any liability, in terms of inattention or otherwise, by any usage or abuse of any policies, processes, or directions contained within is the solitary and utter responsibility of the recipient reader. Under no circumstances will any legal responsibility or blame be held

INTRODUCTION

Thank you for purchasing this book!

My primary intention is to serve you through this book by giving you clear and useful information. My focus is on helping you understand the rare qualities of empaths, their challenges, and their gift. **In this book, I have outlined many ways for empaths to protect themselves from negative energies and to feel happier by getting rid of negative thinking, anxiety, and stress in general.**

One of the main things about this book is that it has useful and practical information. I have not included unnecessary fluff, as I value our time tremendously. There is no point in stuffing this book with hundreds of pages of useless information about topics not directly related to helping you.

As a result, this book is filled with actionable tips and suggestions, and also useful explanation about the key concepts without being a 400-page book. To me, the point of writing a book about a specific topic is to provide the best information on that topic itself (even if that means that my book is smaller in size to other books out there). The main objective of my writing is to help my readers in the most effective way possible, rather than give them a massive book filled with generic information.

Additionally, **I have also included actionable survival tips to help empaths deal with negativity, difficult situations, and people.**

Even if you do not practice all the techniques listed in this book but start implementing only a few of them, you will notice a positive difference in your life. You may also be encouraged to dive deeper into meditation or exercise. The important thing is that all of these techniques have many benefits, and will have a positive impact on your various areas of your life.

MY STORY

Prior to finding out that I was an empath, I went through life with a good amount of challenges. I could not figure out why. I had a very difficult time in most social gatherings and large groups of people. I consistently avoided crowds, and what were fun times for my friends were very difficult times for me.

Then, as I started paying close attention to the people around me, I found out that hardly anyone else was as sensitive. Things that upset me did not upset others; things that were obvious to me were not obvious to others. It is at this point; I started looking into it deeper and found that there were other people with similar qualities and experiences, and they were called empaths.

I cannot begin to tell you how many things in my life suddenly began to make sense. I was constantly told that I 'think too much' and 'feel too much' or that 'I was very sensitive', but for the first time I knew that it was not wrong or bad to have these qualities.

I faced many challenges while growing up and even as an adult. I especially had a difficult time while working a job where empathy was considered as a weakness. Many things in my life started to make sense only after I had learned how to manage my intense feelings as an empath.

If I had the information and skills outlined in this book when I was growing up, I would have made many different decisions. I hope that by reading this book, you or someone you love can feel better, and make decisions that help them thrive as an empath.

Let's Get Going...

I am sure that this book will give you new strategies, tips, and ideas that you can use, and have a positive impact on your life.

You can use this information on a daily basis, and even make it a part of your lifestyle.

The main thing for you to do is to read this book, identify the strategies that resonate with you and then apply those strategies immediately. Applying this knowledge by taking action will make all the difference.

Let's get right into it...

TABLE OF CONTENTS

SECTION 1 UNDERSTANDING EMPATHS

Before we delve into the details of how to thrive as an empath, it is important to understand empaths and their traits.

This section includes information about:

- What is an empath?

- Self-test to find out if you are an empath

- Traits of empaths

- Benefits Of Being an empath

CHAPTER 1

WHAT IS AN EMPATH?

An empath is a person who knows and can often feel what another being feels. Without knowing or understanding why this is just how empaths are. They simply possess high levels of empathy. People often think of empaths are people who are compassionate, but in reality, empaths are not just compassionate, they are **extremely** compassionate since they can feel the emotions and feelings of others.

Empaths are often also called 'Highly Sensitive People' (HSP), but there is a difference. Though HSPs can be empaths not all HSPs are.

It can be said that all empaths are highly sensitive, but not all highly sensitive people are empaths. Here is the difference...

AN HSP is often sensitive and reactive to the energy in their surroundings. Dr. Elaine Aron (the originator of the term), describes it this way:

"A Highly Sensitive Person (HSP) has a sensitive nervous system, is aware of subtleties in his/her surroundings, and is more easily overwhelmed when in a highly stimulating environment."

Even though all empaths are extremely sensitive to energy, the difference is in their gift to perceive and feel another person's real feelings. This ability makes empaths extrasensory as they can directly experience the feelings that are going on within another person.

Even while an HSP has a sensitive nervous system, they do not necessarily possess extrasensory perception. AN HSP may be very sensitive to the energy around them, but they do not connect to other's people's energy the same way. HSPs cannot literally feel what another person is feeling, but instead, they can relate to the feelings of another person. At times, painful emotions get triggered in HSPs when they relate to another person. This is energy that was stored within them, as a result of something that happened in their own past.

Empaths, on the other hand, have empathic abilities that are extrasensory in nature. Many empaths often take in the feelings and emotional energies of other people, which results in a lot of confusion and challenges for them.

This is especially true when a person does not know that they are an empath, and they can shield themselves from feeling too intensely. In my case, I had no clue what was an empath, and that there are many other people who have a similar ability.

Besides having the ability to feel energies intensely, empaths are extremely intuitive too. As a result, empaths are often accurate when they feel something about a person. They do not even have to know a person to get a sense of how that person is feeling.

Empaths, who do not know who to manage the energies and emotions they soak in, can become isolated to guard themselves against the feelings of others. This is not good for empaths, as it frequently leaves them feeling unhappy.

In addition to feeling the emotions of other people, empaths are also very good at understanding the motivations and objectives of other people. They possess an innate sense of 'what is going on' around them.

Now that you have an understanding about empaths and some of their abilities, let us get into finding out if you or someone you love is an empath.

CHAPTER 2

ARE YOU AN EMPATH? TAKE THIS SELF-TEST & FIND OUT

Answer the questions listed below to test if you are an empath. The key here is to answer questions without spending too much time thinking about the response. Simply, go with the first response that comes to mind.

Are you extremely sensitive?

Do you feel emotions intensely?

Do you get affected intensely by the pain of others?

Do you feel overwhelmed and drained in large crowds and social gatherings?

Do you have strong gut feelings and intuition?

Are you very good at listening and find it easy to do so?

Do you feel overwhelmed easily / often?

Do you often think about what others think?

Do you often think about how others feel?

Are you often told that you are sensitive?

Do you notice small details that others usually miss?

Do you tend to consider others first in your decisions?

Do you find it is not easy for you to say, 'No'?

Are you good at picking up mistakes?

Do you prefer to be alone?

Do you avoid noisy and crowded places?

Do you avoid confrontations intensely?

Do you find yourself crying often?

Do you have a creative mind?

Do you enjoy spending time in nature?

If you answered 'Yes' to all or most of these questions, then it is highly likely that you are an empath.

In the next chapter, I have listed the top traits of empaths.

CHAPTER 3

TRAITS OF EMPATHS

Here is a list of the top traits of empaths. Go through this list to see if these resonate with you.

Extremely Sensitive:

By their very nature, empaths are extremely sensitive. They feel bad even for strangers or just by listening to or reading the news. This makes them very nurturing because of their very caring nature. At the same time, they can be easily offended and feel bad often as the people around them are usually not as sensitive.

Very Intuitive:

Being tuned into subtle energies and feelings, empaths are usually very intuitive. Once they learn to trust their intuitions, they can take advantage of this ability in many areas of their lives (like work, relationships, etc.).

Alone Time Is Important:

Empaths have to process through a ton of data that comes in the form of thoughts, feelings, and emotions. Since they are hyper sensitive to the world around them; they may find that their energy gets drained faster than others. As a result, they need more alone time to recharge.

Often Give Too Much:

Since empaths can relate to others and often even feel their feelings, they have a tendency to give too much in their relations and interactions with the people in their lives. Empaths should be aware and careful of this tendency of giving too much, as this can often lead to people taking advantage of them.

Very Generous:

Being generous comes naturally to empaths. They constantly work to help others improve their lives. Empaths are usually very generous with their time, energy, money and other resources. They often operate from the mindset of helping others.

Natural Knowing:

There are many times that empaths know stuff naturally. This knowing is not just an intuition but often much deeper than that. There are many things that seem just obvious to an empath, which is not the case for almost everyone else.

Picking Up Dishonesty Easily:

It is almost like there is a detector for lies somewhere in the minds of empaths. They can easily spot lies. It is also very easy for them to pick out people who tend to say one thing but mean something else.

Creative Beings:

One of the gifts that an empath has is abundance is their creativity. Empaths usually have a vibrant imagination. This helps them be very creative and they can often be good at writing, acting, making music, painting, etc.

Introverts

Many empaths are introverts. They prefer to interact with people in small groups or even one – on – one. Often, they feel drained and overwhelmed in large crowds.

Absorb Other People's Energy & Emotions:

Empaths naturally pick on the moods and emotions of the people around them. So, if they are around people who feel negative emotions often, they can tend to take these negative emotions on themselves. This is particularly difficult for most empaths, as they often feel emotions intensely. They also get positively affected by the positive emotions of the people in their surroundings.

Constantly Feel Tired:

Empaths feel drained and overwhelmed more easily than many others, as they tend to take on too much from others. Also, empaths tend to attract energy vampires, who add on to this feeling of tiredness.

Have An Aversion To Clutter:

Since empaths feel things more intensely than most people and also tend to pick up on subtle energies, it is natural for them to enjoy a space that is clean and clutter free.

Exceptional Listeners:

It is innate for empaths to care for others. This quality makes them very good listeners, as they genuinely care about others and their well-being.

Enjoy Spending Time In Nature:

The chaos and busyness of a fast paced city can be overwhelming for empaths. They tend to find relief and peace in nature. Spending time in nature is a good way to recharge for empaths.

Attracted To Healing & Holistic Therapies:

Most empaths are natural healers. Empaths are naturally drawn to learning about and using healing and holistic practices, as they are genuinely interested in healing others. Even though helping people comes naturally to empaths, many find it hard to become healers because they tend to take on too much emotion and feeling from others, and thus overwhelm themselves.

Can Appear Moody Or Reclusive:

Feeling emotions intensely makes empaths susceptible to mood swings, as their feelings can change rather easily. An empath can be feeling relaxed and happy one moment, and then feel quite sad and unhappy upon watching the news or hearing about any negative event.

This tendency to feel sad easily makes some empaths withdraw from social situations and they tend to become reclusive. It is easier for them to be by themselves than to be with many people around and risk feeling bad.

Suppress Their Emotions:

Many empaths push down their own feelings and emotions, even though they are very good at listening to and helping others. They feel that they may be burdening others by unleashing their own emotions and feelings. In some cases, they also do not want to be told that they are 'too sensitive' or to 'toughen up'.

Unfortunately, most of our society looks at sharing emotions and feelings as weakness. Often, people who are sensitive are told that they are 'too sensitive' with the connotation that their sensitivity is a weakness. This is one reason that many empaths do not like sharing their feelings and emotions with others.

CHAPTER 4

BENEFITS OF BEING AN EMPATH

Empaths face many challenges due to their ability to feel other people's emotions and feelings intensely. As a result, they may forget that there are benefits to being an empath.

Some of these gifts possessed by empaths are so innate and obvious to them that it feels natural. Empaths feel that everyone must be able to understand or know what they know. It is only after observing others astutely; they may realize that their abilities are real gifts that only a few possess.

High Degree Of Understanding:

Empaths are sensitive to the subtleties that most people miss, and so they are excellent at perceiving all kinds of hints and nonverbal communication easily. This provides them with the gift of understanding others without having to be told explicitly.

Good At Picking Up Lies:

Empaths are also very aware of people's feelings, emotions and thoughts. This helps empaths to pick up on lies easily. In many cases, they can tell when a person is lying to them, even if they have never met the person before.

Extremely Creative:

Creativity is another gift that empaths possess. Empaths have a tendency to think differently and so can imagine things that others cannot.

Feel Good Easily:

It is a tremendous gift to be able to feel good easily. Some empaths may think that life is more challenging for them, as they feel negative emotions easily. In reality, empaths feel positive and negative emotions easily. Many people are not able to feel much when they listen to a song or have a delicious meal, while empaths can feel really good simply by having an experience they enjoy (like listening to a song they like, spending time in nature, etc.).

Empaths do not need much to feel good and can do so even without any company. While most people need to be at a party or traveling or shopping to feel good, empaths feel good without needing much. A walk in nature or a funny movie can feel just as good as spending time with an old friend.

Avoid A Lot Of Trouble:

Since empaths are highly intuitive beings, they end up avoiding a lot of mistakes and chaos in their lives by simply trusting their intuitions and making the right decision. I cannot list how many times; this one ability has helped me personally. I have avoided trouble several times and in many forms by trusting my intuition. Additionally, I have also been able to help family members make good decisions based on my intuition. This is true for most empaths I know.

Are Natural Healers:

Empaths are naturally aligned with healing others. Many empaths use this ability to help others by learning healing techniques like Reiki, Acupuncture, Reflexology, Crystal Healing, etc. There are also a number of empaths who are drawn towards psychotherapy, counseling, etc.

Connect Easily With People:

It is much easier for most empaths to connect with others. Others may have to go through extensive training to learn what comes naturally to empaths, in terms of connecting with people. Empaths can often even connect easily with strangers. This makes it advantageous for empaths to do well in jobs where they need to connect with others, especially in small groups or on a one – to – one basis.

Very Nurturing:

Many people find it difficult to comfort others in times of difficulties, while empaths can do so without much trouble. This is the main reason that people often turn to empaths when faced with a crisis. Having this ability to help loved ones to deal with a difficult time is another one of empath's gifts.

Good At Manifesting Desires:

Manifesting goals can be easier for empaths, once they learn to let go of the negative energies in their life. Since empaths feel very strongly, they can manifest their desires easily by focusing on them and letting go of any resistance in the form of negative energies.

SECTION 2

TYPES OF EMPATHS

Being an empath comes with its own set of challenges and gifts. Not all empaths are the same, as there are essentially six different types of empaths. By understanding the type of empath you are, you are in a position to make the most of this gift while minimizing the challenges you face.

Even though there are six different types of empaths, you may find that you have characteristics of different ones. Empaths do not necessarily belong to just one category or type.

CHAPTER 5

EMOTIONAL EMPATH

The majority of Empaths is emotionally receptive, and can physically and emotionally sense the feelings coming from other people before they are even conveyed.

The emotional empath is one of the most typical types of empaths. This most common type of empath simply gets the emotional states of others near them and experiences the results of all those emotional states, as if those emotions were their own. The emotional empath will intensely have the feelings of other people inside their own personal emotional body.

An emotional empath can easily come to be deeply distressed, especially when they are around people who are in an intensely negative emotional state. To put it simply, the emotional empath will feel the negative feelings of the other person in a negative state and relate to their problems and discomfort.

For emotional empaths, it is essential to learn to distinguish between their personal sentiments and those of others. This way, emotional empaths can utilize their ability to help others without being depleted or becoming depressed themselves.

Lots of empaths really feel drowned by this specific capability, since they can really feel the energy of a space as soon as they walk into it.

An empath varies from a Clairsentient since the clairsentient feels the emotional states of other people without taking on those emotional states themselves. The empath, however, takes on other people's emotions, deeply experiencing them within their personal emotional system.

With skill, the empath can alter their empathetic power into the clairsentient ability by disallowing other people's emotions to affect them.

CHAPTER 6

PHYSICAL EMPATH

People with this type of empathy have the ability to pick up on the energy from other people's bodies. They can intuitively feel and find out what ailment is troubling the other person. In many cases, they may even feel strong sensations and discomfort in their own body. In some other cases, they may be able to 'see' the blockages in another person's energy field.

As a result of these capabilities, these types of empaths make for good healers, and many of them actually become healers and medical professionals.

These type of empaths may not only feel sensitive to other people's emotions but may actually even feel their pain. If you are this type of an empath, it would be beneficial to study energy healing, to ensure that you do not take on the pain and ailments of others. Also, it would be useful to be able to clear and even strengthen your own energy field prior to working on healing another person.

CHAPTER 7

INTUITIVE EMPATH

In case you are an intuitive empath, you will be able to pick up information about people by being around them. These types of empaths are also called, 'Claircognizant' empaths.

It is very easy for these types of empaths to detect when someone is lying to them, as they are good at picking up the intentions behind people's words and actions. They can usually tell a lot about a person by simply looking at them, even if they have never met the person before.

This ability is a very useful gift, as these types of empaths can avoid all kinds of trouble by being able to tell when someone or something seems 'off'.

It is recommended for these types of empaths to strengthen their own energetic field too, as they may get bombarded with thoughts and emotions from others.

CHAPTER 8

GEOMANTIC EMPATH

Geomantic empathy is often also called place or ecological empathy. This is a fascinating one since people with this capability are tuning into the earth in a way that they can notice and look out to pending natural catastrophes like earthquakes, floods, hurricanes, etc.

People with this type of empathy and ability have a great attunement to physical landscape. In case you feel uncomfortable or actually happy in specific places or locations, for no evident reason, then you are likely a geomantic empath.

If you are a geomantic empath, you may also feel a deep connection to certain locations. Location empaths are extremely attuned to the natural world and feel sad when any damage is done to it.

CHAPTER 9

PLANT EMPATH

A plant empath is a person with a close association with plants or flora species. If you are a plant empath, you intuitively sense what plants need. A plant empath definitely can notice a plant's requirements, such as where a plant may want to be placed.

If you are this kind of an empath, you will already know that you require a lot of contact with trees and plants. You may prefer to enhance this bond by sitting quietly by a special tree or plant and attuning more closely to its needs and guidance. This makes plant empaths naturally good at gardening.

Even though this skill is represented in fiction as a magic power, a lot of typical people are plant empaths and plenty more might open this ability with a little practice.

Many plant empaths have an affinity with specific types of plant life. Plant empaths are able to know what a plant requires and may not enjoy being close to a plant that is passing away or that needs water.

It is said that a plant empath can often communicate with plants intimately. Anil Ananthaswamy in his essay, "Roots of Consciousness", mentions that plants are aware of their environment and even other plants around them. In addition to being aware, it has been found that plants can also communicate what they perceive.

CHAPTER 10

ANIMAL EMPATH

Lots of empaths have a strong connection with animals. Animal empaths are those who understand what it is like to be an animal. Those with this gift will understand what an animal requires and may be able to telepathically communicate with the animal.

An animal empath will probably dedicate their lives to working for the care of our animal friends. If you are an animal empath, you probably already invest as much time with animals as you can. You might find that studying the biology or psychology of animals interests you. You might also consider training as an animal therapist, as your special talent can allow you to discover exactly what may be troubling an animal and treat it accordingly.

Animal empaths make great vets and vet nurses (although some empaths may feel too sensitive to work in these occupations.) They might likewise opt to work with animals in the capacity of animal therapists.

This ability to be able to understand the feelings of animals enables an animal empath to explore the animal's emotions, worries, and feelings. The majority of animal empaths have a special affinity with a particular of animal, like dogs, cats or even snakes, as animal empaths are not necessarily drawn to all animals.

These are the six main types of empaths. In the next section, you can find information about strategies to help you protect yourself and your energy as an empath.

SECTION 3

PROTECTION STRATEGIES & SURVIVAL TIPS FOR EMPATHS

Being an empath is a gift but it often does not feel like it. Most empaths struggle with relationships, work and just interacting with people in general. This can be changed by proactively learning about the steps to take to protect and heal yourself as an empath.

In this section, there are 16 different strategies to help you thrive as an empath. You may find that some of these strategies resonate more with you than others. If this is the case, then you can focus on using those strategies first.

1

THE FIRST STEP TO THRIVING AS AN EMPATH

ACCEPT THE CHALLENGES & GIFTS OF BEING AN EMPATH

"The more you know who you are, and what you want, the less you let things upset you."
Stephanie Perkins, Anna and the French Kiss

The first step in thriving as an empath is acceptance. It is not easy being an empath, even though it has many benefits. Most empaths have a difficult time in their relationships, work, social situations, etc., as they can easily feel low and discouraged.

Life becomes much easier once a person becomes aware of their qualities and abilities, and accepts them for what they are. It is natural for most people to resist what they do not like, but what we resist often persists in our lives. By letting go of any resistance one may have towards their abilities as an empath, they can begin to deal with any situation in a healthier manner.

The key in these situations is to look at this ability for what it is by learning about it. Being an empath has its pros and cons, just like most things. Once it is understood what these pros and cons are, it is much easier to navigate through life by avoiding the pitfalls.

2

THE SECOND STEP TO THRIVING AS AN EMPATH

RELEASE NEGATIVE THOUGHTS & FEELINGS REGULARLY

"Try giving up all the thoughts that make you feel bad, or even just some of them, and see how doing that changes your life. You don't need negative thoughts. All they have ever given you was a false self that suffers. They are all lies."
Gina Lake, What about Now?: Reminders for Being in the Moment

One of the biggest challenges faced by empaths is that they tend to feel bad easily and often, as a result of their heightened sensitivity to energies. This often results in empaths feeling low or depressed, especially if they do not proactively work on releasing the negative energies they take in.

We live in a world that seems to be filled with negativity, and this makes it very difficult for empaths to be happy and at peace. It may feel like there is too much wrong with the world around us or just too much negativity in general. Even though it is impossible to avoid suffering and negativity forever, it is very helpful for empaths to learn how to release any negativity that they may be feeling.

Be releasing the negative energies that enter the body and mind, empaths can feel more positive, energetic and peaceful. If such energies are just let be, they can occupy a person's mind and body for years.

How To Release Negativity?

It took me a long time to learn this. To release negative energy, follow the steps outlined here:

Accept - When you realize that you are feeling any form of negative emotion, simply accept it. Accept that there is this negative feeling or sensation without judging it or resisting it. This may be easier said than done but it helps tremendously to objectively acknowledge what is.

Observe - Now, observe this feeling or sensation in your body. Where do you feel it in your body? Is it a painful feeling or a heavy feeling, etc.? Notice your thoughts as well. What are your thoughts saying? Simply watch your thoughts and feelings without getting involved, as if you were watching a movie. When you observe your thoughts and feelings in this manner, you start dis-associating with them without even trying to change them.

Release – Now simply release this energy. Let go of this energy. Take some deep breaths, and when you exhale just say, "I bless and let go of this energy that I am feeling." This may feel counterintuitive or you may simply resist blessing something that is troubling you, but this is a good way to let go of things that may have bothered you.

I started releasing negative energy using this technique, and it made a massive difference to my life. I used this technique every night, and sometimes even a few times a day. Letting go of negative energy in this way takes only a few minutes at a time, and by proactively doing so, I started making sure that I did not keep suffering bad feelings for a long time.

This is one of the most important strategies that I have learned as an empath. By actively releasing any stored negative energy, empaths gain more control over their own feelings and emotions.

3

HOW TO PROTECT YOURSELF FROM BEING OVERWHELMED

SET LIMITS AND BOUNDARIES

"No is a complete sentence."
Anne Lamott

One of the main reasons that empaths suffer is because most of them lack strong boundaries. It is not their fault because they feel emotions so intensely; often it is difficult to know which emotions are theirs.

In many cases, people around empaths notice their tendencies to constantly help people feel better, which encourage some of them to take advantage of empaths. It is common for empaths to place others' needs before their own, and even though this is a very noble act, it often leads to people manipulating empaths. Be aware of such people in your life, as they may constantly come to you for help, even when they could do without it.

To safeguard their own health, well-being, and peace of mind, it is extremely important for empaths to be comfortable with saying 'no' to people. **Keep in mind, that you cannot share what you do not have,** and so it is of utmost importance to look after yourself first. There is nothing wrong with caring for your own well-being first.

It is not your duty or responsibility to act as a sponge by taking in negative energies from others. Setting strong and healthy boundaries is a requirement to thrive as an empath.

If there are people in your life that feel stressed or negative easily and often, it is important to remind them to focus on the positive and to have an attitude of solving their problems. It does not help anyone to continually focus on problems and to keep complaining about them. If they stick to complaining, then cut them off politely and take care of yourself first.

4

HOW TO KEEP YOURSELF FROM GETTING DRAINED

IDENTIFY DRAINS & ENERGIZERS

"Every time you feel depressed about something, try to identify a corresponding negative thought you had just prior to and during the depression. Because these thoughts have actually created your bad mood, by learning to restructure them, you can change your mood."

David D. Burns

A crucial step in managing the challenges of being an empath is to identify what drains your energy and what helps you in feeling energized. Once, an empath has better insight into people, places, events and situations that drain energy and ones that energize them, it becomes much easier to be selective in their day to day life.

Equipped with this knowledge, empaths can avoid everything that drains their energy or makes them feel negative emotions. They can also use this information to intentionally spend more time on things that energize them.

Once a person finds out about their empathic abilities, they can take this as the first step in their journey to managing their abilities. Most empaths feel confused and drained because they skip this step. Once, they find out what helps them and hinders them as an empath, they can find more peace and positivity in their lives.

5 - HOW TO PROTECT YOURSELF FROM OTHER PEOPLE'S ENERGY

VISUALIZE A SHIELD AROUND YOU

"Your spirit is the true shield."
Morihei Ueshiba

This is a popular technique to help empaths. When you are in a situation like social gathering, work meeting, etc. that you would like to avoid but cannot, it may be helpful to visualize a shield around you in the form of a bubble. You can even think about it as a bubble of light.

You can choose what you let in this shield and what is left out. In this way, you can imagine letting only the good in while letting anything negative stay out. If you feel that your energy is getting drained, you can block the negative person draining you.

This technique takes a bit of practice for one to get used to. However, this technique does not resonate with some people as they find it hard to visualize things.

6 - HOW TO CUTDOWN NEGATIVITY

AVOID NEGATIVE MEDIA

"If people in the media cannot decide whether they are in the business of reporting news or manufacturing propaganda, it is all the more important that the public understand that difference, and choose their news sources accordingly."
Thomas Sowell

A lot of the news, movies, shows, music and other forms of entertainment and information have become quite negative over the years. There just seems to be a consistent supply of negativity through the media in today's world.

Though many people may not see it that way, empaths know exactly what I am talking about. Since empaths are hyper sensitive and can feel things easily, it is best for them to avoid this bombardment of negativity. It would be highly beneficial for empaths to avoid taking in too much negative information, as this has a serious impact on their emotional state.

It is better to skim through a news website to stay in the know, rather than sit in front of a news program that would unleash segment after segment of negative news for hours on end.

It is also a good idea to watch 'feel good' movies and shows, as this will actually have a beneficial impact on empaths. Empaths can enjoy such movies and shows more, as they feel positive emotions more easily too.

7 - LIGHTEN UP TO FEEL BETTER

AVOID THE TEMPTATION TO TAKE ON TOO MANY RESPONSIBILITIES

"The first step towards true enlightenment is to lighten up on yourself."
Bashar

It is good to be in a position to be able to help people in their time of need. This is a good ability to have but as mentioned previously, it is most important to take care of ourselves first.

Most empaths feel the need to constantly help the people in their lives while ignoring their own needs. Even though this mindset leads to the benefit of other people, empaths end up paying the price for this. If you find yourself in a situation where you could help someone, it is important to not take on too much responsibility and feel drained or depleted in the bargain.

In reality, people are responsible for their own lives. I do not mention this as an attitude of indifference but to point out that at the end of the day, each one of us is responsible for taking care of ourselves. By constantly giving too much to others, empaths have a tendency to become depleted and suffer themselves. Remember, you cannot give to others what you do not have yourself.

Stick to taking care of yourself first, even if someone does not like you putting yourself first. In case you would like to help others, you can have a limit in terms of how much you will help.

8 - HOW TO HEAL AS AN EMPATH

FORGIVE

"Life is so short. The only person you hurt when you stay angry or hold grudges is you. Forgive everyone, including yourself."
Tom Giaquinto

Forgiveness seems to be a simple concept but it is one of the most transformational actions that a person can take to improve their lives. True forgiveness takes place when a person genuinely lets go of the negative energy (in the form of thoughts and feelings) about a person, situation or event that they were holding on to.

Till a person proactively forgives another person or situation that caused them pain or suffering, they end up holding on to negative thoughts, feelings and emotions about it. Since most people are not as sensitive as empaths, it is likely that empaths often find themselves in situations or around people that offend them. When this happens, it can feel very hurtful to empaths and can make them feel low.

If you hold on to the hurt feelings, your energy will get drained. This makes it important to realize that you have the power to forgive others and feel better yourself, as a result. Another important part of this process is to learn from such experiences and set strong boundaries. These steps will help you prevent such events from repeating.

9 - HOW TO PREVENT ABSORBING PEOPLE'S NEGATIVE ENERGIES

MOVE AWAY

"It is by choice and not by chances that we change our circumstances."
Nadia Sahari, Breakaway: How I Survived Abuse

Empaths can also take on people's energy by simply being physically close to them. This makes life quite challenging for empaths living or working in crowded cities. The fact is that it is extremely difficult, if not impossible, to avoid large crowds for long periods of time (unless you live and work in a remote place).

Even though it may be difficult to completely avoid large crowds, it would be beneficial to move away from energy vampires as much as possible. If you get a negative feeling or sensation whenever you are in close proximity to a certain individual, leave that space and move a bit further. The more you increase your physical distance from such people, the better you will feel.

10 - BE SELECTIVE TO BE HAPPY

CHOOSE YOUR FRIENDS PROACTIVELY & LET GO OF TOXIC RELATIONSHIPS

"You're going to come across people in your life who will say all the right words at all the right times. But in the end, it's always their actions you should judge them by. It's actions, not words, that matter."
Nicholas Sparks, The Rescue

Many people do not pay much attention to the company they keep. They come across people in their day to day lives and become friends with some of them. This may work for many people but it is not ideal for empaths. Empaths have to be more guarded than others to protect themselves from negative energy and feelings.

The people in our lives make a big difference to us. We are constantly affected by their energy, attitudes and mindset, and vice versa. As an empath, if you have friends or family members who tend to be negative, then you become susceptible to constantly taking in that negative energy and suffering as a result.

You can safeguard your health, happiness and peace of mind, by proactively selecting positive people as friends. By doing so, you will be able to keep the negativity away, and also flourish as a result of the positive energy in your life.

Be sure to fill your life with supportive and encouraging people. It is not worth holding on to relationships with the hope that someday the person will change for the better. Those who genuinely want to change will do so proactively.

Even though this attitude of letting go of negative people from your life may seem cold, it is not. It is a practical way to ensure that you do not keep suffering as a result of other people's actions, words or energy.

11 - HOW TO STAY POSITIVE EASILY

SAY YOUR AFFIRMATIONS

"Affirmations are our mental vitamins, providing the supplementary positive thoughts we need to balance the barrage of negative events and thoughts we experience daily."
Tia Walker, The Inspired Caregiver: Finding Joy While Caring for Those You Love

Being an empath, you may feel a lot of negative energy in your daily life. It is not easy to go through life being constantly bombarded with negative thoughts and feelings. To counter this, it is important to focus your attention on the positive in life.

Saying affirmations daily are a simple way to focus your attention on the good in life, especially when you get a lot of negative thoughts. This may not be easy in the beginning but with some practice, it becomes easier to center yourself using affirmations.

The first thing to do, in order to make the most of this strategy, is to make a list of some powerful affirmations that resonate with you. Then, schedule 5 – 10 minutes every day to say these affirmations. Also, use these affirmations when something or someone triggers negative thoughts in you.

12 - REFRAME YOUR WAY TO PEACE

REFRAME YOUR OPINION OF OTHERS

"Opinions do not have to be permanent. It is helpful to look at things from different perspectives to get a fuller understanding."

Vik Carter

As an empath, it may be confusing and difficult for you to watch others behave in ways that are hurtful. You understand intuitively that it is not good to behave in such a way but many others do not.

This can lead to developing a negative opinion towards many people in your life, and holding this opinion against them. Remember that not everyone is intentionally hurtful or negative. Many people are simply this way because of their mental and emotional conditioning, and may not even realize that they are being hurtful.

So, it is best to look at people who act negatively as ignorant rather than negative. By making this change, you will be able to forgive them and not hold on to a negative image of them. This will also help you in releasing any negative energy you may take on from them.

13 - HOW TO RELEASE NEGATIVE THOUGHTS & FEELINGS

EXERCISE

"Take care of your body. It's the only place you have to live."
Jim Rohn

Being highly sensitive, you may feel quite overwhelmed with all the thoughts and feelings that you have to process every day. This can cause fatigue and frustration, if not managed proactively.

A good way to release extra energy in the body is through physical exercise. It can be through running, weight lifting, cross fit, yoga, cycling or any other form of physical exercise that resonates with you. This may have multiple benefits for you as an empath. You will improve your health, and release any toxic energy in the process.

In addition to releasing any toxic energy from your body, you may also find clarity in your thoughts and mind, as a result of exercising regularly. This is also a good way to spend some time alone. You can simply go for a run by yourself or go to the gym at a time when it is empty.

NOTE: The next 3 tips are Bonus Chapters From My Book 'Declutter Your Mind'

14 - HOW TO FIND MORE PEACE IN YOUR LIFE

MEDITATE - MEDITATION IS THE OPEN SECRET THAT BRINGS PEACE AND CALM INTO OUR MINDS AND LIVES.

Practicing Meditation is an excellent way for empaths to stay grounded, as meditation relaxes the body and mind, and helps to heal from mental and emotional stresses.

"Meditation can help us embrace our worries, our fear, our anger; and that is very healing. We let our own natural capacity of healing do the work."

Thich Nhat Hanh, The Miracle of Mindfulness:
An Introduction to the Practice of Meditation

Over thinking is quickly becoming the norm in our society, as the pace of modern life continues to increase. We are surrounded by automation and gadgets, and still, have to play catch up with everything that is happening around us. In addition to the increasingly fast pace of life, we have our pasts to deal with, the many things in our futures to worry about and maybe even some challenges to overcome in our present. No wonder, our thoughts and minds get filled with clutter easily and often.

Whether it is relationships, work or just keeping up with day to day life, it is becoming increasingly difficult for most people to keep up. What most people do not realize is that we are living in a world of extremes. There are too many choices, too many decisions to be made, too many things to look into, too many messages to answer, too many tasks to finish and so on.

One of the most effective ways to declutter our minds of negative thoughts and emotions in this fast paced world is meditation. People have practiced and benefited from meditation for thousands of years, and there is a simple reason for that....it works!

My journey towards decluttering my thoughts and mind began with my practice of meditation. Many years ago, I would get stressed and worried easily and as a result feel negative emotions often. To overcome the negative

thoughts and emotions that kept filling my
mind, I started meditating. This one step to
protect myself from regular negative thoughts
and emotions has literally changed my entire
life for the better.

What Is Meditation?

There are many definitions of meditation,
depending on the type you are practicing;
however, several forms of meditation focus on
training your mind to be aware of the present
moment and to pay complete attention to it.

Meditation is a practice of turning your
attention inward and putting your attention on
a single thought, breath, feeling or sensation.

How To Meditate?

Follow these steps, to get started with meditation:

Find a quiet and comfortable room where you can practice meditation for 15 – 30 minutes at a time without being disturbed.

Sit in a comfortable position.

Close your eyes, and focus on your breathing. You do not have to alter your breathing to make it deeper. Just breathe naturally, and put your full attention on it.

After a few breaths, you may notice your mind being distracted by thoughts. Do not worry or think that you are failing at meditation when this happens. You can expect this to happen, as your thoughts have a lot of momentum.

Whenever you get distracted by thoughts, simply bring your attention back to your breathing. That is it. Keep bringing your attention back to your breathing. This is the practice of meditation.

It may take some time to focus your attention on your breathing for longer amounts of time. This is natural. The important thing is to practice daily without worrying about the results. By being disciplined in your practice, you will notice that you are able to focus on your breathing and meditate more easily.

This is the simplest form of meditation, and very popular for beginners. You can always learn about the different ways to meditate and practice the one that resonates with you.

In my opinion, meditation is the cornerstone for having a clear and focused mind. Having a daily meditation practice is one of the best things that you can do for having a peaceful and decluttered mind, and to get rid of negative thoughts and emotions that may be clogging your mind. This practice of meditation will also improve your overall health.

Benefits Of Meditation

A study done by the University Of Massachusetts Medical School has demonstrated that meditation can enhance a person's overall brainpower.

Meditation boosts productivity and promotes focus, according to a study conducted by the University of Washington.

There have been other studies that have shown how meditation can improve the symptoms of anxiety and depression, help preserve the aging brain, and help with addiction.

There is also a study published in Brain Research Bulletin that backs the claims that meditation can lead to reduction in stress.

There are many studies (in the hundreds) published in various scientific journals showing that meditation, when practiced regularly, can be helpful in managing, preventing and coping with a variety of physical and mental health issues.

These include:

- Anxiety

- Insomnia

- Depression

- ADHD

- Asthma

- Chronic pain

There is also research that indicates meditation can help improve DNA repair and boost immunity.

Is Meditation Only For Religious People?

Many people think that meditation is a religious practice or for Buddhists and yogis only. This is not true. People all over the world, from all walks of life, are practicing and benefiting from meditation.

Even though there is a strong association of meditation with religion and spirituality, you can choose to view it as an exercise for your mind or simply a practice to help you stay grounded as an empath. Meditation is simply a practice, and anyone can do it without changing their religious views or beliefs.

The interesting thing is that meditation is widely practiced by elite athletes, biggest movie stars, musicians and even Wall Street tycoons. In short, some of the most successful people on the planet also practice meditation. I have heard interviews of some of the most successful hedge fund managers saying that they meditate daily.

Also, some people think that meditation is odd or difficult, but it is actually fairly simple (that is the whole point, right ☺). Just like anything else, it takes a little bit of getting used to, and the key is to not get discouraged in the initial stages. If you keep practicing on a daily basis without getting discouraged, it will become an anchor for you.

When I started practicing meditation, I could barely sit still for a few minutes. Now, I practice meditation 2 to 3 times a day. It may only be for 10 minutes at a time but it has become an important part of my daily schedule because of the massive benefits I have seen as a result of practicing it.

Empaths can benefit greatly from a regular meditation practice, as it will help them stay grounded in times of emotional turbulence.

"Meditation is painful in the beginning but it bestows immortal Bliss and supreme joy in the end."

Swami Sivananda

RECOMMENDED READING:

If you would like to learn more about meditation, the following 2 books are my picks.

My favorite book for decluttering the mind and protecting ourselves from negative thought is **The Untethered Soul by Michael Singer**, who has been featured and interviewed by Oprah. This book is also a New York Times Bestseller with more than 1 Million copies sold.

The Untethered Soul is a must read for anyone interested in finding more peace of mind, and protecting themselves from negative thoughts and emotions.

Real Happiness is also a New York Times
Bestseller and one of the best books on
meditation.

15 - HOW TO FEEL MORE POSITIVE & ENERGETIC

PRACTICE DEEP BREATHING - BREATHE DEEPLY TO CALM THE MIND AND TO LET GO OF EXCESSIVE THINKING

"For breath is life, and if you breathe well you will live long on earth."

Sanskrit proverb

Breath is vital to life. It is the very first thing we do when we are born and the last thing we do before leaving from this life. It is estimated that during our lifetimes, we take approximately half a billion breaths.

What we might not recognize is that the mind, body, and breath are completely linked and affect each other. The way we breathe is influenced by the thoughts we think, and our thoughts and physiology can be directly impacted by our breath.

Deep breathing is often used to calm the mind, and can be a precious tool in helping to restore balance in the mind, and body.

Scientists have actually documented the advantages of a regular practice of basic, deep breathing that include:

- Lowered stress

- Increased levels of energy

- Reduced depression and anxiety

- Muscle relaxation

- Reduced feelings of stress and overwhelm

Most people are unaware of the impact of breathing on their emotional states. Breathing is an extremely powerful technique to control our mental and emotional states.

You may have noticed that our breathing patterns change with a change in our mental and emotional state, but may not know that we can control our mental and emotional states by proactively choosing the way we breathe.

By taking deep breaths, our bodies relax and minds become calmer. Breathing can have an instant effect on diffusing emotional energy, and thus is a great way to release negative energy from our bodies. It is also a very effective strategy for empaths to let go of tension and stress when they feel overwhelmed.

One of the most effective ways to let go of negative thoughts and emotions, and to get energized is through the practice of deep breathing. This focused deep breathing results in relaxing muscles, reducing your heart rate and calming the mind.

Deep breathing puts our attention back on the mind and body, and energizes us. We become more aware of what is going on inside our mind, as our mind becomes quiet. It is easier to become aware of the clutter and negativity in our thoughts when we breathe deeply.

By practicing deep breathing, we can let go of this cluttered thinking and gain more peace and harmony in our minds and lives.

The changes that occur physiologically as a result of deep breathing are referred to as the "relaxation response." The relaxation response is an expression that was first made by Dr. Herbert Benson. Dr. Benson describes the relaxation response as, "*a physical state of deep rest that changes the physical and emotional responses to stress... and the opposite of the fight or flight response.*"

Dr. Herbert Benson wrote a book called 'The Relaxation Response', in which he outlines the advantages of several relaxation techniques in treating a number of stress-related disorders.

Regular practice of deep breathing has numerous health benefits, in addition to decluttering the mind and grounding us to the present moment. Following are some of the benefits of deep breathing:

Relieve Stress

Deep breathing leads to a relaxation of our mind and body, which in turn leads to relieving any stress stored in the body. As we let go of the stress felt by us, we feel more relaxed.

Stabilize Blood Pressure (Or Even Lower It)

When we breathe deeply from our abdomen, it encourages a complete exchange of oxygen, which is the helpful trade of inbound oxygen for outgoing co2. This can result in the lowering (or stabilizing) high blood pressure.

Reduce Pain

Deep breathing brings in increased levels of oxygen to the body, which is needed by most cells in the body. The oxygen assists in removing the neurotransmitter within the blood and reduces pain that is caused by blood circulatory problems.

Increased Energy

The level of energy we have throughout the day depends on our breath to a large extent. The fuller our breath, the more energy we will have. By taking deep breaths, we get more oxygen into our bodies, which in turn increase the amount of energy we have.

How To Use Deep Breathing To Feel Better?

Follow these steps to establish a daily practice of deep breathing.

Decide a time of day that would be best for you to take 5 – 10 minutes to practice deep breathing. You can also add 5 minutes to your meditation time, and begin with 5 minutes of deep breathing. This will help your meditation practice, and you will not have to allocate separate times to meditation and deep breathing.

Find a comfortable and quiet place where you could easily sit and practice deep breathing. You can leave your phone and other gadgets out of this room.

Sit in a comfortable position. You can sit anywhere (chair, floor, bed, etc.) or even lie down. Just make sure that you are in a comfortable position, and do not have to keep moving during your practice.

Many people think that it is not good to lie down, but I have found that it is okay to do so, as long as you do not fall asleep. If you find that by lying down, you feel drowsy or sleepy, then it is best to sit up during your practice.

Close your eyes, and breathe in deeply through your nose. Inhale as much as you can comfortably without overdoing it. Hold your breath for a couple of seconds.

Exhale slowly all the way. Hold your breath for a couple of seconds before taking your next breath.

Spend just 5 to 10 minutes daily breathing deeply, and focus your attention on your breath while you do this. This is a very helpful technique in taking your attention away from a racing mind.

If you notice that your attention goes towards your thoughts when you do this, simply bring your attention back to your breathing. Do not get upset or impatient, if this happens. Just keep bringing your attention back to your breathing and keep breathing deeply till you have done so for at least 5 minutes.

Another tip is to gradually increase the amount of time you practice deep breathing. You can get started with 5 minutes, and then keep increasing by a couple of minutes every other week till you can easily practice deep breathing for 15 to 20 minutes.

This practice is very effective for clearing your mind. Also, you should feel more relaxed within minutes of doing this practice.

What I like most about this technique is that you do not need to be in a special setting to do this. You can practice deep breathing in your car, in a park or while waiting for something, in addition to doing so at home. I usually do so whenever I find myself waiting...like at the barber shop or a doctor's clinic.

Keep in mind that a routine practice of deep breathing is one of the very best tools for improving your health and well-being. It is recommended that you practice deep breathing twice a day for at least 5 minutes at a time.

You can also use this technique to calm yourself any time you start feeling stressed or negative. By training your body with a regular practice of deep breathing, you will start to breathe better even without concentrating on it and will find it easy to let go of stress, anxiety and other negative emotions with this simple technique.

"One way to break up any kind of tension is good deep breathing."

Byron Nelson

RECOMMENDED BOOKS:

Breathing: The Master Key to Self Healing by Dr. Andrew Weil. Dr. Andrew Weil says, "If I had to limit my advice on healthier living to just one tip, it would be simply to learn how to breathe correctly."

16 - HOW TO RECHARGE YOUR BATTERIES

SPEND TIME IN NATURE

"Keep close to Nature's heart... and break clear away, once in awhile, and climb a mountain or spend a week in the woods. Wash your spirit clean."

John Muir

Empaths connect deeply with nature. This is one of the easiest ways for empaths to recharge themselves, and so it is a good idea to take some time every couple of days to spend at least a few hours in nature.

A walk by the beach or in the park does wonders to soothe the mind and help us get away from our day to day activities. Spending more time in nature may also improve the way our brains work and improve our mental health, according to a study of the physical effects of visiting nature on the brain.

Since most people live in cities today, we do not end up spending much time in nature. Being away from the daily hustle has its perks, which may mean an increase in our mental peace.

Studies show that people who live in cities tend to have a higher risk of depression, anxiety and other mental illnesses as compared to people who live in smaller towns.

The events of people living in cities not spending much time in nature and having a higher risk of depression and anxiety seem to be related to some extent, according to an increasing body of research.

A variety of studies has found that urban dwellers with little access to green spaces have a higher rate of psychological trouble than people living close to parks. It is also found that city dwellers who visit and spend at least some time in nature have lower levels of stress hormones immediately afterward than people who have not recently been outside.

As an empath, one of my favorite ways to declutter my mind of all negative and emotional thoughts is to go to the beach, and simply walk. I make it a point to not listen to music or speak on the phone when I do this. The whole point of doing so is to not engaging my mind in the usual stuff but instead to take a breather from day to day things, and simply watch my thoughts.

I have also noticed that when I use this strategy of just allowing myself to rest by spending time in nature without clogging my mind with thoughts of all the things I need to do that day, I usually get a lot of good ideas for my business. It is almost as if my mind frees up to let new ideas come in during this time. If this happens, I simply record my ideas on my phone and then work on them when I get back to my office.

This technique is very simple but effective. As a side benefit, you may get a bit of exercise too while walking along the water.

You can also choose to go to a park or go for a hike. Do whatever suits you most but the key is to get some quiet time and unwind.

CONCLUSION

Congratulations on completing this book! We have covered a lot of practical information in this book. We have discussed many effective ways to protect yourself and thrive as an empath.

Most people buy books but never end up completing it. They put off reading the book or even if they read it they never complete any of the exercises or go through any practice.

By practicing what you have learned here, you will start seeing results in a short span of time, and once you see positive results, you will be encouraged to keep implementing these strategies. It is imperative to not get discouraged in the process, and to keep practicing till you see the results you want.

I wish you much success in using this rare gift and thriving as an empath!

MORE BOOKS BY VIK

1. **DECLUTTER YOUR MIND NOW** - 22 Simple Habits To Declutter Your Mind & Live A Happier, Healthier And Stress-Free Life

2. **MINIMALIST LIVING** - 33 Minimalist Lifestyle Habits To Declutter Your Home, Save Time And Money & Live A Meaningful Life - A Guide To Minimalism

3. **HOW TO TALK TO ANYONE ANYWHERE** – 23 Simple Tips To Talk To Anyone With Confidence, Start Conversations And Connect Instantly

THANK YOU

THANK YOU for downloading my book! **I wrote this book with the intention of serving you.** So, if you enjoyed this book or found it to be useful, I would highly appreciate your feedback.

Please leave me your REVIEW on Amazon (no matter how short – even a few words or your STAR RATING would help ☺)

Your feedback is very important and will help me continue to write the kind of books that help you get results.

It has been a pleasure serving you and will keep doing so in the future.

Yours in friendship,

Vik Carter

<

36796898R00076

Printed in Great Britain
by Amazon

36796898R00076

Printed in Great Britain
by Amazon